# An EDITOR LOOKS at RUSSIA

## ONE UNPREJUDICED VIEW OF THE LAND OF THE SOVIETS

### by *Ray Long*

RAY LONG &
RICHARD R. SMITH, INC.
NEW YORK · 1931

COPYRIGHT, 1931, BY
RAY LONG & RICHARD R. SMITH, INC.

———

*All rights reserved*

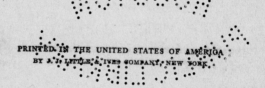

*To my son,*

RAY LONG, Jr.,

with envy for the fact that he
will live to see so much more
of what will happen in Russia
than I possibly can.

MOST of the books which have
been published about Russia
have been written by persons who sought
to prove something. Some sought to
prove that Russia under the Soviet is a
land of despair and failure; others that
it is a land of hope and success.

I went to Russia with no preconceived
notion of what I was to find and with no
desire to prove anything. I went pri-
marily to get acquainted with some of
the Russian writers of today and if possible to find material of theirs which
would appeal to the public in the United
States and England.

I was tremendously interested in seeing
the workings of the Soviet system, but I

was neither pro-Soviet nor anti-Soviet. I still am neither pro nor anti, but I have come to certain conclusions which may be of interest, and possibly of importance, to my fellow countrymen.

You will not find in what I have written any attempt at profound study of the political situation in Russia. Rather you will find an effort to picture the country in the terms of human beings with whom I talked and whom I studied; in the terms of my own experiences and my own reactions.

I met pretty much the sort of folks you would meet if you visited Russia today, and I had, in all likelihood, much the same sort of experiences that you would have. And, therefore, I shall write as if I were taking you as a companion on my trip.

I think you will agree, when we have finished, that it is the most interesting journey one may make anywhere today, and that the experiment being made in Russia is the most fascinating human experiment—and certainly the most important—of our times. Indeed, in its effect on the world at large, it is probably the most important human step since the birth of Christianity. It is moving with the speed of cinema projection, and, no matter where it may end, it is certain so vitally to affect you and me and our neighbors, that it is wise that we study it carefully and intelligently.

Come, then, let us be on our way.

## CHAPTER
### ONE

I ENTERED Russia in October, 1930. I wanted to be in Moscow in time for the celebration of the thirteenth anniversary of the Revolution. I left Berlin on a cold, clear autumn night and my first impression of what was ahead of me was far from pleasant.

With some friends I had dined at the Esplanade and one of the friends— James R. Quirk, a publisher—accompanied me to the station. As we drew near the Square in front of the banhof, we heard a roar like surf beating on a beach. The Square was packed with people, mostly young people. As our taxi edged its way through the crowd someone started singing The Internationale.

Hundreds of voices took it up and the chorus must have been heard blocks away. There was much more of threat than of music in it.

The porter who took my bags to the train platform explained that several hundred young Communists of Germany were to go to Moscow by the same train as I to take part in the celebration. The others had come to see them off and had taken the occasion for a Communistic demonstration. They contented themselves with speechmaking and singing; and so far as we could see they were not molested by any of the numerous policemen who were mingling with the throng.

I was wearing a fur-lined overcoat with a large fur collar—a coat which I had purchased a number of years before in New York but had worn so seldom that it looked practically new. I confess that I must have looked quite a lot like

[ 2 ]

the opulent figure which Communistic cartoonists use to represent the capitalistic class. I offered an aggravating contrast to the poorly clad Communists.

As the train drew in to the platform, the young Communists in the crowded coaches which had been attached to the end of the train began hurling all sorts of imprecations at me. They were so violent in their language that Mr. Quirk became apprehensive for my safety and begged me not to go on that train. I decided, however, that there was no more danger on it than on any other train, so I settled myself comfortably in my compartment and waited for something to happen. Nothing happened. Presently I went to bed and had one of the best night's sleep I ever had on a train. When I arose next morning I found that the two coaches of Communists had been detached at Warsaw. They were to proceed to Moscow by some other train.

[ 3 ]

That's one of the surprising things about Russia: you get worried about a lot of things you think are going to happen and then nothing does happen. It's the things you don't anticipate which disconcert you. For instance, I expected difficulty getting into Russia. I had none. True, I could not get a passport visa in the United States, since we have no relations with the Russian government; but I got one without difficulty in Berlin. Yes, it was easy to enter Russia; but to leave, that was another matter, as you shall see.

I had heard some rather weird stories of experiences of Americans in crossing the border, so as we approached Nigeroyle, the first point across the line, I was a bit nervous. In addition to my ordinary luggage, I had with me a large package of food—tinned chickens and hams, baked beans, coffee, canned fruits and the like—as a precaution against the food shortage in Moscow. There was a cursory examination of the luggage on the Polish side of the border; then we proceeded to Nigeroyle. It was a little after four in the afternoon, but already darkness was falling. The customs house was a poorly lighted, long, low frame building. I looked about for a porter to carry my bags. There was none in sight. I started toward the building, staggering under the weight of the luggage, when from somewhere a husky, broad-shouldered chap, in the ordinary costume of blouse, heavy trousers and boots, sprang out of the dusk, grabbed the load of bags and marched into the sheds, as if they were no heavier than a paperweight.

I spoke no Russian, so my first task was to find an interpreter. There was only one, and there were many demanding his assistance. When I did get him, however, my troubles all seemed to vanish. In fact, if my experience may be taken

[ 5 ]

as a criterion, the stranger entering the gates of Russia gets considerably more of courtesy than does the stranger entering a number of other countries, including our own. But, always remember, leaving is another matter.

I had been advised to register the amount of American and German currency which I was carrying. This is an essential precaution, because when you depart from Russia you must account for all that you have spent and must show receipts for all the currency which you have changed into Russian money. The amount which you have spent must be sufficient to satisfy the officials that you have used each day an amount which would enable you to live on the scale that your position should warrant. All this seems a lot of useless red-tape at first, but it is understandable when you realize that the Soviet government values rubles at two to the dollar and *redeems* all that you have in your possession at departure at that rate. If you exchange your money in the legitimate way, through your hotel or through the State Bank, you get only two rubles for the dollar, but—and here is the reason for the precaution—it is possible to buy bootleg rubles at as many as eight for the dollar almost anywhere in Russia. And, obviously if the government redeems any bootleg rubles at that rate it is doing a losing business.

The answer to the bootleg rubles is that most of the people have accumulations of money. Their incomes exceed their possible outgo. True, wages are low, according to American standards. But there is no unemployment; in fact, there is a great shortage of labor. As a result, all the members of a family work. And what they may spend of the wages they receive is determined by the government. Each has a ration card, and he may not buy more than the card allows. And often he may not buy that, for so scanty has been the supply of food and clothing that much of the time it has been impossible to fulfill the card allowances.

Since for all practical purposes there is no form of entertainment on which the money may be spent, it accumulates. The government endeavors to get the people to put their accumulation in the State savings bank but this effort isn't very successful. The result is that the workers will take the chance of underselling the government in its own currency because they feel that no matter what happens, American money, or even German money, will have a value always, whereas if there should be a successful counter-revolution the ruble may not be worth anything.

After my luggage had been passed and I had registered my money, I found the

[ 8 ]

same porter and got him to help me get my luggage to the train. He did so rather grudgingly (which is not an unusual attitude on the part of porters), but when he had completed the task he gave me a surprise.

I had been busy putting some bags into a rack overhead. When I got down and looked around to tip him he was nowhere to be seen. I stood beside the coach, assuming, of course, that he would come back for his tip but up to the time the train pulled out there had been no further sign of him. This was the first time in my life a porter ever failed to collect. When I got to Moscow next day my friends there explained this phenomenon. The porters are paid by the State. They are not supposed to take tips. They are expected to be—and apparently are—self-respecting working men who earn their salaries and do not depend on the charity of passengers. Quite a contrast to Italy and some parts of France, where 10 per cent is added to your bill for gratuities, but where, if you fail to slip at least as much more into the palms of the servants you get little service and much ill luck.

## CHAPTER TWO

BEFORE the train started, the conductor demanded my passport—and calmly put it in his pocket. Well, I'm like most Americans traveling abroad. As long as I have my passport, I feel comfortable; but once it's out of my possession, I get nervous. I tried to protest, but it didn't avail me anything. I realized that he probably hadn't the slightest idea of what I was saying, so I resigned myself to my fate.

One can realize that in the old days travel on Russian railroads must have been the most luxurious in the world. In the first place, the Russian railway tracks are wider gauge than those in other countries. This plan was inaugurated as

[ 11 ]

a precaution against invasion by Poland or other countries to the south. If the invaders brought troops by train to the border they must proceed from there on foot because their standard gauge trains could not operate on the Russian tracks.

My compartment seemed to be almost half again as large as a drawing-room in an American Pullman. Instead of the berths being lengthwise of the coach and one above the other, the lower runs cross-wise of the compartment and the upper lengthwise, which gives a degree of comfort impossible in our style of coach. There is one disadvantage, however. A single passenger may not buy both of the berths and one never knows until one gets on the train just what sort of companion one may draw for the trip. This sometimes proves embarrassing, because the Russians have no prejudice against putting a strange man and woman in the same compartment.

My room mate from the border to Moscow was a Frenchman who was on his way there to represent an engineering firm. He knew a little English and I speak a little French; each of us had a smattering of German, so that between the three languages we got along quite well. As a matter of fact, when we went in for dinner we got almost chummy because each of us was defeated in his effort to masticate the steak which was served as the principal part of the meal.

We began with a watery vegetable soup. It developed to be practically the only food we could eat on the entire menu. The meat was so tough that I don't believe any human being possibly could have chewed it. It was called beef but we both were quite certain it was beef taken from an overworked cabhorse that had died of senile debility. However, we did have a bottle of very good Armenian wine and between it and the black bread we got enough so that we didn't suffer.

My friends in Moscow had advised me to arrive at least one day ahead of the day of celebration, and next morning I realized how wise they had been. We have overcrowded cities in the United States at times, but we never had anything to compare to Moscow. Literally, it would have been almost impossible for me to get from the station to the hotel had I waited until the following day. As it was, there was not the slightest possibility of getting a taxi and even to have found an unoccupied drosky might have been difficult. However, Walter Duranty, correspondent of The New York Times, had sent his Ford to the station and in it we piled my food, luggage, two other men and myself and got away looking like a party of tin-can tourists in the United States.

And when we arrived at the Grand Hotel, I learned that I had been lucky in getting a room. It had been possible only because an American engineer who had occupied a room for several weeks had been called away for duty in the Ukraine.

There was one American woman—an ardent Communist at home—who failed to get a room at all. Not only at the Grand but in any other hotel. She spent the nights on a couch in the home of a friend, and when I met her later, her ardor for the Cause was considerably dampened. Considerably.

I found when I registered that I must surrender my passport again. (It had been returned to me by the conductor as we pulled into the station.) This time the head porter of the hotel took it; and I didn't see it again until I left Moscow. This is a simple means of keeping a check on your movements, for of course you can't travel anywhere without a passport.

[ 15 ]

The rate for my room was 36 rubles a day, which in American money is $18.00. Naturally, for that price I expected something rather luxurious. Instead, I was led to a room about eighteen feet by twenty, barren of carpets, with two plain chairs, an exceedingly plain table, a wardrobe and two iron beds of a sort that one could find only in a junk shop in the United States. The windows looked out on a court and the roof of another section of the hotel came to within a few feet of the window ledge. This did not please me greatly because I had visions of intruders finding it easy to enter the room, but I soon realized that they wouldn't have such an easy time because these were double windows and they were sealed for the winter. The only way to get any air into the room at all was through a little slot about a foot long and three inches wide. The result was that at all times there was an

[ 16 ]

odor in the room much like that in a Chinese laundry.

There was a small wash basin but of course no bath. I found later that there was one bath in a suite on each of the floors, which of course was for the private use of the occupant of the suite, and one public bath tub to each floor. I took one look at the one on my floor and decided that if I was expected to use it I should go unbathed throughout my stay in Moscow.

However, I was in luck. The suite on my floor was occupied by Junius B. Wood, correspondent of The Chicago Daily News, and he invited me to visit him each morning for my shave and bath. He went farther in his kindness. He had provided himself with an electric hotplate and was one of the few persons in Russia who had coffee for breakfast. Had I been dependent on the hotel for breakfast, all that I should have been able to get would have been two thin slices of black bread and a glass of tea. Wood, however, lived in luxury. With him each day I shared not only the coffee but a plentiful supply of black bread and generous portions of caviar. The average American stomach probably would be revolted at caviar for breakfast, but I state as one who knows that after the first day or two it becomes a delightful breakfast dish.

I found that my precaution in bringing a supply of food had been wise. Even at a hotel like the Grand the menu is extremely limited and to the American palate decidedly unattractive. In the first place, Russian cooks drown food in grease. So that the two or three ragouts on the menu each day—and that's about all there was—were not only made from meat you scarcely could eat, but had been treated in such a manner that they couldn't have been likable, even had the meat been good. I was able on two or three occasions to get ham and eggs in the hotel restaurant, but I soon found that the way for me to live comfortably was to impose on the generosity of my friends.

Most of those friends were correspondents for American newspapers and press associations. They manage to live quite comfortably. Each of them requires an office in addition to living quarters, so each of them adopts the plan of having his office in his home. Wood's suite at the Grand was adequately furnished and well carpeted. One or two other correspondents lived at the hotel but most of them had apartments in other parts of the city. Eugene Lyons was especially comfortable, as he had one floor of what had been almost a palace. The others had somewhat smaller places but the House Commission of the government does see to it that the correspondents may live without undergoing the hardships of the average Russian family. There is a shop where only foreigners may buy and the supplies of food there are more plentiful than in the shops maintained for the Russians, and also a shop for clothing is maintained exclusively for foreigners.

However, let me illustrate the difficulty in getting clothing. I wanted to purchase a real Russian blouse. There was none to be had in the shop for foreigners. I asked Mr. Duranty's chauffeur to go to the shops for the workers. He canvassed the entire city and was unable to find one. I also endeavored to purchase a woolen hunting blouse as a protection against the cold and could not find one anywhere. Neither could I purchase the materials to have one made.

I adopted the plan of breakfasting with Mr. Wood, lunching with one of the other correspondents and dining with still another, and in this way got along quite well. I distributed the tinned foods which I had brought with me among those on whose generosity I was living and everything seemed to work out satisfactorily for all of us. We didn't live opulently, but we lived well and in grim contrast to those we saw about us.

This was despite the fact that on account of the celebration of the anniversary of the Revolution, the government had provided extra supplies for the workers and had made extra allowances, especially of boots. As we would leave the comfortable homes of my friends, we would see lines of patient people waiting in front of the State supply shops. This went on all through the day and through most of the night. At three o'clock one morning I saw a line that seemed to me almost as long as the line which I had seen in front of that shop at noon of the preceding day. My friend,

Eugene Lyons, told me that by waiting, each of those in line might get as much as two pounds of bread a day, half a pound of meat, a little sugar, a bit of tea, once in a great while a few eggs, and about half a pound of butter a month. Not much food is it? And yet there is no question of starvation when one may have that much.

And, there you come to one of the phases of the Russia of today which is almost impossible of comprehension to the person who has not seen the country with his own eyes. You naturally would think that a people compelled to endure those hardships in order to get food or clothing would be so dissatisfied as to be in a mood for revolt. But what you must do in order to understand their stoicism under such circumstances is to compare what they endure today with what they endured in the old days.

They may have to wait until three

o'clock in the morning to get food or
boots today, but under the Czars they
were lucky if they got enough to keep
body and soul together at any time and
most of them never owned a pair of
boots. They protected their feet from the
cold by wrapping them in straw bound
with rags. And after all, if you never
had owned a pair of shoes in your life,
you wouldn't feel it such a great hardship to stand in line for hours to get a
pair. And, if you had never known what
it was to have a comparatively full stomach, you wouldn't quarrel with a government which saw to it that you did get
enough food to prevent hunger, even
though it made it difficult for you to get
that food.

This is the first fact which impressed
itself on me in Russia. The people there
are living under conditions which to an
American working man would represent
the extreme of poverty and hardship, but

those conditions are so much better than those under which the Russian worker lived in the past that to him they represent almost luxury.

In addition, the Soviet system has given the Russian peasant and the Russian worker something which he never had before: Hope.

The Russian is told day after day and day after day that while things are bad now, he must consider himself part of an army fighting a war against Capitalism and that when that war is won, all shall share in the benefits. He is promised a day when each worker shall have a comfortable home, plenty of food and plenty of clothing.

And, there is no question that each month under the present system he gets a little closer to that goal. He cannot aspire as yet to homes with bathrooms, radios, pianos or any of those things which are a part of the life of the American worker. But he scarcely knows of the existence of such things. He does aspire to comfort and unless something upsets the machinery that now is in motion I can't see any reason to question that eventually he will get it.

I want to recapitulate what I have said above because to me it seems so essential that anyone trying to understand Russia —and I think it is of vital importance for all the rest of the world to begin to understand Russia—must appreciate the fundamental facts.

You have a country living in hardship, living under the strictest governmental control of any country that ever existed, a country in which liberty as we understand the word is utterly impossible; a country in which the citizen does the work which he is told to do for a wage in the determination of which he has no voice, and yet a country in which the citizens seem to be more nearly contented than in any other country I have seen in the world today. And the most vital factor in that contentment, I believe, is the fact that Russia is a nation in which for centuries the great majority of the people not only practically were slaves but certainly were hopeless. Take a man who has had no hope for the future and give him hope for the future and you have given him something more valuable than anything else in the world. And no matter what else Communism has done for the Russian it has given him Hope.

## CHAPTER THREE

T HE Soviet government is doing one of the most efficient jobs of advertising to sell that factor, Hope, that any organization ever has done. It is advertising an ideal—a social, a political and an economic ideal—directly to the consumer, the 160,000,000 people of Russia. The government advertises to them every minute of every day. It uses billboards, posters, newspapers, magazines and the radio; the theatre, the motion picture, even the opera and the ballet.

Throughout Russia you see billboards, but those billboards are not carrying announcements of tires or automobiles, of skins-you-love-to-touch or cigarettes to keep you kissable. They are advertising

Communism. They tell the peasant what he may hope for under Communism. They also tell him in bold letters, "If you do not work, you do not eat." And that is meant literally. That's why Russia has no leisure class.

On the blank walls of buildings you see posters. Here again you find no effort to sell commercial products. The posters advertise the union of the worker and the farmer and the soldier. They advertise the promise of the Five-Year Plan. And there is one, a vivid red and black color scheme, which shows a bolt of lightning striking squarely into the head of a cringing figure. The lightning is the all-powerful O.G.P.U.—the secret service of Russia. The cowering figure is that of a counter-revolutionist. And, believe me, after you have met that poster face-to-face a dozen or more times during the day you get the feeling that being a counter-revolutionist is not healthful—decidedly not.

All the newspapers and all the magazines in Russia are owned by the State. Of course, practically everything in Russia now is owned by the State but the control over all the avenues of publicity is more strict than it is over any other line of endeavor. It was my observation —and this observation was confirmed by the correspondents—that the censorship on news which is to go to the outside world is not nearly so strict as you might have believed. The Soviet censors don't seem to care so very much about what the outside world thinks of Russia. They not only permit the foreign reporters to send their own views of whatever facts may transpire, but they put unusual facilities at their disposal.

For instance, on the day of the Thirteenth Anniversary, the chief censor made his headquarters at Junius Wood's apartment in the Grand Hotel. All the other correspondents came there and prepared their articles. The censor did what editing he wanted to do without forcing them to take the manuscripts through the crowded streets to the postoffice.

Likewise, on the day when the arrests were made which led to those recent trials—then again he came to the Grand Hotel and edited the copy there. I looked over some of the articles which were sent. For all practical purposes, he had not changed them at all. A word here and there, a sentence here and there, but nothing had been done to prevent the correspondent conveying to his readers his personal viewpoint or interpretation of what was happening.

That doesn't prevail for the Russian newspapers. Of course, there is little necessity for censoring them because they are all managed and edited either by members of the Communist party or by men so clearly in sympathy with the movement that they ask nothing better than an opportunity to publish propaganda. The result, of course, is that 90 per cent of the reading matter in the newspapers and magazines is direct propaganda.

It is as if the Republican party owned and edited all of the newspapers and the magazines in our country. You can imagine how little criticism there would be of Mr. Hoover in any of the papers or magazines. Senator Borah would have slight chance of finding his name in any of those papers. And can you imagine the space Franklin Roosevelt or Al Smith might get?

Then the radio. This seemed to me in some ways the most effective medium of advertising which the government was using. At intervals of two or three blocks, loud speakers have been placed along the streets of Moscow and Leningrad. No matter in which direction you may be going you hear throughout the twenty-four hours, coming over the radio, arguments in favor of communism, explanations of its shortcomings, stories of the accomplishment of the Five-Year Plan, and so on. Those voices are in your ears when you get up in the morning and they are there when you go to sleep at night.

Sometimes one doesn't sleep so well at night in Russia. I had one night in Moscow when I think I lost about two years' growth.

Junius Wood and I had dinner at the home of Walter Duranty. After dinner we sat around with some good port and talked about Russia in general, but particularly they were telling me stories of the O. G. P. U.

The secret service under the Czar was powerful, but the secret service under the Soviet is so much more complete, so much more powerful that as between the two there is no comparison.

The foreigner visiting Russia has the feeling that his every move is being watched. I don't credit the stories of dictaphones in all the hotel rooms, for the simple reason that I don't think there are enough stenographers in Russia who understand English to make a record of the conversations in English which go on in the Grand Hotel alone. But, you do suspect that your waiter, the chamber-maid—every person in the hotel—is an agent of the O. G. P. U. You realize that no matter how carefully you may lock your luggage, they find keys to unlock it. This is so true that I finally quit locking mine because I didn't want the locks injured.

But to go back to that night. Wood and I left Duranty's about midnight and came back to the Grand Hotel by tram car. It was an interesting ride because

[ 33 ]

it was just at the time the workers of the midnight shifts were going to their jobs. The street car was as crowded as a New York subway express at nine in the morning. We were jammed in among a lot of folks who didn't seem to enjoy our presence particularly, so when we got to the hotel I heaved a sigh of relief. I went to bed immediately and read for fifteen or twenty minutes, then turned off the light.

Just as I was dropping off to sleep I had the feeling that someone was watching me through the window. I turned on my side to look. Sure enough, there were two luminous eyes boring right in at me. I turned back, not feeling at all comfortable, but deciding I had to find out something about this thing, I turned on the light again and pretended to read for a few minutes and then looked at the window. There was nothing there. I waited a little while, then extinguished

[ 34 ]

the light again. But this time I lay on my left side and faced the window. Within a few seconds there came those eyes again. It seemed to me they were looking straight into my soul. By that time it was easy for me to believe they were full of malignant hatred. I reached up over my shoulder, snapped on the lights again,—and found myself looking straight into the face of the biggest tom-cat I ever saw. It had come up over the adjoining roof and climbed onto the window sill.

My nervousness that night was a result of the advertising of the O. G. P. U. It had sold me the idea that if I didn't watch out I was liable to be snatched out of my bed and stood up against a wall so that some of the Soviet soldiers might practise marksmanship on me. Yet the chances are that I was as safe in Moscow as I am any day in New York. In fact, with our traffic and racketeer problems in

[ 35 ]

New York, I probably ran less chances of injury or death in Moscow than I do in New York.

Traffic is one problem they don't have in Moscow. There are less than a thousand automobiles in the entire city, and only a few taxicabs. The taxis are owned by the State and are remarkably cheap —if you can get one. But the trouble is to get one.

There being so few taxis, the person who gets up earliest and gets one of them, keeps it for the entire day. If one has to take a drosky, the price is terrible. For a ride of a few city blocks the fare will be from five to six or seven dollars. This is because the drosky driver is a man without citizenship. He is a private owner and private owners have no standing. They get no ration cards, and therefore they must buy the necessities for themselves and for their horses from other private traders. One drosky driver told my interpreter that it cost him $12.00 a day to feed his horse. In spite of this, the horses looked to be in good condition. The carriages were not. Apparently none of them has been repaired since the Revolution. As you go bumping over the cobble-stone pavements you have the feeling that any moment you are liable to be pitched out. As a matter of fact, later in the winter, when they use the narrow-bodied sleighs, it is not uncommon to see a passenger catapulted from one of the sleighs into the snow.

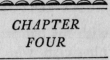

IN contrast to your drosky driver, is the man who works with his hands. He gets "all the breaks." His ration card entitles him to food and clothing ahead of any of those who do not work with their hands; and his children are the first to gain entrance to the schools.

The distinctions between the various grades of workers must have been evolved by a genius. For instance, I was told that in the breadshops the man who sells bread by the loaf is not a black worker and therefore is not in the most favored category. But the chap who cuts loaves of bread and sells sections of them is a black worker and is in the most favored category. A surgeon is a worker

[ 38 ]

with his hands; he is a black worker; a physician who writes prescriptions, or gives you medicine, is not.

There is no category in which there is luxury. But if the ideal for which Russia is striving works out, the class which will get luxuries first will be the class that works with its hands; the class that never had luxuries. That is the foundation of Lenin's philosophy and of the creed of Joseph Stalin, his successor. The aims and methods of Stalin were explained so clearly by Walter Duranty in a recent article in the New York Times that instead of trying to explain them myself, I have gained his kind permission to quote him.

"Stalinism," he said, "is a tree that has grown from the alien seed of Marxism planted in Russian soil, and whether Western Socialists like it or not it is a Russian tree.

"Old Russia was an amorphous mass,

[ 39 ]

held together by a mystic, half Asian idea of an imperial regime wherein the emperor was exalted to the position of God's vice regent, with limitless power over the bodies, souls, property and even thoughts of his subjects. That, at least, was the theory, and it was only when the Czars themselves began to question it and 'act human' that a spirit of doubt and eventual rebellion became manifest.

"The Czarist regime was poisoned by the European veneer that was spread over Russia—a veneer that was foreign and at bottom unwelcome to the mass of the Russian people—and one of the things the Bolshevist revolution did was to sweep away this alien crust and give the essential Russianinity underneath an opportunity to breathe and grow. Which explains why the Bolsheviki, who at first were a mere handful among Russia's millions, were able successfully to impose their dominant principle — namely,

Marxism—which in superficial appearance was far more alien than the Germanized or Westernized system it overthrew.

"The truth is that the ideas outlined in the Communist Manifesto of Marx . . . suited the Russian masses much better than the Western theory of individualism and private enterprise imported by Peter the Great and his successors, who finally perished in the conflict it involved with the native character of Russia.

"Lenin took and shaped Marxism to fit the Russian foot, and although circumstances compelled him to abandon it temporarily for the New Economic Policy, he always maintained that this political manœuvre was not a basic change of policy. Sure enough, Stalin, his successor and devout disciple, first emasculated the NEP and then set about abolishing it. Today the NEP is a sorry slave in the outer courts of the Soviet palace.

"That is what Stalin did and is doing to our boasted Western individualism and spirit of personal initiative—which was what the NEP meant—not because Stalin is so powerful or cruel and full of hate for the capitalist system as such, but because he has a flair for political management unrivaled since Charles Murphy died.

"Stalin is giving the Russian people . . . what they really want, namely, joint effort, communal effort. And communal life is as acceptable to them as it is re-pugnant to a Westerner. This is one of the reasons why Russian Bolshevism will never succeed in the United States, Great Britain, France or other parts west of the Rhine.

"Stalinism, too, has done what Lenin only attempted. It has re-established the semi-divine, supreme autocracy of the

[ 42 ]

imperial idea and has placed itself on the Kremlin throne as a ruler whose lightest word is all in all and whose frown spells death. Try that on free-born Americans, or the British with their tough loyalty to old things, or on France's consciousness of self. But it suits the Russians and is as familiar, natural and right to the Russian mind as it is abominable and wrong to Western nations.

"This Stalin knows and that knowledge is his key to power. Stalin does not think of himself as a dictator or an autocrat, but as the guardian of the sacred flame, or 'party line,' as the Bolsheviki term it, which for want of a better name must be labeled Stalinism.

"Its authority is as absolute as any emperor's—it is an inflexible rule of thought, ethics, conduct and purpose that none may transgress. And its practical expression finds form in what is known

[ 43 ]

as the five-year plan. The Soviet five-year plan is a practical expression of the dominant principle—which for convenience the writer will call Stalinism, although Stalin still terms it Leninism—which rules Russia today with absolute authority.

"In a sense it is far more than a plan—and in another sense it is not a plan at all. It is a slogan for a national policy and purpose rather than the glorified budgetary program which it appears at first sight to be. [Most persons outside Russia seem to think that if the five-year plan 'fails' it will be the end of Bolshevism and that if it 'succeeds' it will mean the end of capitalism elsewhere. Nothing could be more absurd or more wrong.

"The five-year plan is nothing more or less than applied Stalinism, and its mass of bewildering figures is only the thermometer to measure the degree of heat

[ 44 ]

engendered by the application of the plan, but it is not otherwise intrinsically important. The figures have been changed so often and so considerably as to cease to have real value save as an indication of the 'tempo,' or rate, at which Stalinism is gaining ground.

"To the rest of the world it is only a menace, in the sense that Bolshevism itself is a menace—which may or may not be true. To Russia it is only a hope or promise in terms of what Bolshevism itself offers. But to the Russian people the five-year plan is infinitely more besides —it is a goal to aim at, and its inception cannot but be regarded as a stroke of genius by anyone familiar with the Russian nature.

"Russians, ignorant or wise, have a positive passion for plans. They almost worship a plan, and the first thing any one, two or more Russians ever do about anything is to make a plan for it. That, after making his plan, the Russian feels satisfied and seems to lose sight of the fact that a plan must next be carried out is one of the great obstacles Stalin and his associates are now facing.

"So to conceive a whole national policy and everything in the national life as one gigantic plan was the political tour de force that put Stalin in the highest rank. Every one who has employed Russians or worked with Russians or knows Russians finds that if he wants them to jump on a chair, he must tell them to jump on a table, and aiming at the table they will reach the chair. The important thing is that they have something to jump at and make an effort—whether they actually get there all at once or not does not really matter in a country of such vast natural resources and with such a tough and enduring population.

"What matters is that they keep on

trying, and that is what Stalinism and its five-year plan is set to make them do. In other words, the five-year plan is something for the Russians to measure at, not for the rest of the world to measure Russians by. This sounds confusing, but it is true, and if you cannot understand it you cannot understand Russia.

"The whole purpose of the plan is to get the Russians going—that is, to make a nation of eager, conscious workers out of a nation that was a lump of sodden, driven slaves. Outsiders 'viewing with alarm' or hooting with disdain as they take and play with Soviet statistics might as well be twiddling their own thumbs for all it really counts.

"What does count is that Russia is being speeded up and fermented—and disciplined—into jumping and into making an effort and making it all together in tune to the Kremlin's music. That is why the Soviet press utters shouts of joy about the five-year plan for oil production being accomplished in two and a half years and does not care a rap when some meticulous foreigners comment about the fact that nothing like the five-year amount of oil has actually been produced.

"What the Soviet press really means is that in two and a half years the daily production rate—or tempo—has reached the point set for the end of the fifth year of the plan—in short, that Oil has jumped on the table way ahead of time. That the said rate may only be maintained with the utmost difficulty has small importance to Russian logic, and rightly so, because a successful effort has been made and what a man has done once that man can do again.

"Russia and Russians and Russian logic are different but the fact that they are different does not necessarily mean they are wrong."

[ 48 ]

T HE ceremonies to celebrate the thirteenth anniversary of the Revolution gave me an opportunity to study Stalin at close range. It was one of the most interesting days of my life. We had places in the press section with the correspondents and had been told to breakfast early so that we could get to the reviewing stand not later than eight o'clock. After that hour the streets were almost impassable. There was no hardship about getting up early; it was impossible to sleep through the noise of the gathering lines of parade. They began to gather at daybreak and some of those lines were still in formation at midnight when I returned to the hotel.

The parade focused before reviewing stands in Red Square. First came long lines of infantry. There certainly was no indication of starvation on the faces of those soldiers. They were about the finest looking body of men I ever saw, and no army which has come under my observation was as well clothed as the Russians. It has always seemed to me that in providing uniforms of our own army, the tailors assumed that all men were of the same size and same build. In Russia, each soldier looks as if his overcoat had been tailored expressly for him by an expert. Following the infantry, came cavalry, tanks, armored cars, supply wagons and scores of pieces of artillery. There were 30,000 soldiers in line, all of them from the Moscow garrison. Overhead a fleet of forty planes circled. All of these planes were Soviet made. Some of them were big four-motor bombers, so formidable in appearance that they sent shivers down one's back.

Immediately after the soldiers came the delegation of young German Communists and the enthusiasm with which they were greeted must have repaid them for the long journey. Then came files and files of workers—700,000 of them. Here again, instead of a look of starvation the people seemed to be well fed and they certainly were warmly clad. I don't mean to give the impression that they were well dressed according to our standards. Their clothing was poor and in many cases shabby, but I saw none who seemed to be underdressed. I suppose it is true that what they wore that day was their best—perhaps their all—but there was no question that dressed as they were they were fully protected against the weather and it was the sort of raw, snowy, chilly day that is characteristic of Moscow in autumn.

There were squads of school children in the parade and there I got a surprise. I, like you, had read of the gangs of wild children which infested Moscow during the early years after the Revolution. These little ones in the parade were rosy-cheeked, much better dressed than their elders and apparently about as happy a lot of youngsters as you would find anywhere. There is no question that they would compare favorably with the children in the streets of the average factory town of the United States, and more than favorably with the children in English and European factory towns.

There is, of course, a definite reason for this. Everything in the Communistic plan is for the future. A child is much more important to the State than an old person. A child is a potential party worker, a potential contributor to the laboring force of the country. Therefore to the children go the first of the supplies of milk, butter and eggs. They are the country's greatest asset. For the first time in Russian history, their teeth and their health are being cared for and guarded. For the first time, the children of the working classes are being educated. A great proportion of the State's money is being spent for educational facilities. Those facilities aren't sufficient to take care of all, but they are growing; and during the time they are insufficient, the children of the workers get the preference. In other words, if I were a Russian my child could not get an education until all the children of those who work with their hands were taken care of. That, of course, makes it difficult for the families of what in this country we might call the middle classes or the upper classes, but in Russia these comprise so small a part of the population that their hardships do not balance in the scale against the advantage to the workers.

[ 53 ]

There again, you see, is that great factor, Hope. The Russian working classes were almost 100 per cent illiterate in the old days. Today fifty million can read and write; and constantly the State says to the workers, "Your child shall have the sort of education of which you never could have dreamed." There is an element of hope the value of which it is almost impossible to overestimate.

The press stand from which we observed the parade was just in front of the grave of Jack Reed, the American journalist who played such a spectacular part in the organization of the Soviet Republic and who died of typhus while working with Lenin and Trotsky. To our right was the tomb of Lenin, a black and red marble structure built in modernistic fashion. It seems incongruous there in the Red Square with its background of the almost Oriental buildings of the Kremlin. The idea is eventually

[ 54 ]

to destroy all those marvelous old buildings and replace them and their history
with modernistic buildings which look
to the future instead of to the past.

Lenin's tomb was used as a reviewing
stand by Stalin and his aides. Stalin came
to his place by himself. There was no
bodyguard and apparently there was no
precaution taken for his safety. He is a
typical Georgian, Stalin, a striking figure
of a man, broad-shouldered, deep-
chested, easily six feet tall and with a tremendously vital personality. He is
swarthy, black-haired, brown-eyed and
wears a stubby black mustache. He had
on a plain khaki colored uniform and
overcoat with a military cap to match
but with no insignia of rank to be seen.
Most of the officials around him were
dressed similarly and those who were
not in uniform were plainly clothed. I
had to smile when one of the correspondents reminded me of the silk hats that

would have been in evidence at the review of any parade in the United States, and especially in New York. Grover Whalen and his Committee to receive distinguished guests wouldn't have fitted into this picture at all.

While we were in the reviewing stand, I received an invitation from the government to attend that night a reception to the foreign diplomats and correspondents. The reception was to be given in one of the old marble palaces, but the invitations specifically stated that no one should wear evening clothes. This was all right for the men, but it put a difficult problem before the wives. The only sort of informal clothing which they had was street dresses and a street dress in Russia is not in any sense of the word a party dress. All of them had evening gowns, but of course their evening gowns were sleeveless and low-necked. Most of them got around the difficulty by making sleeves and some sort of arrangements to close the necks of their evening gowns, but a number did go in street clothes.

Having as a part of my work attended many banquets of various sorts, I thought that I knew the kind of food that would go with an occasion of this sort. But when, after being received by Stalin and the members of the government, we proceeded into one of the dining rooms— there were three—I saw an array of food which dazzled my eyes. The dinner was buffet and literally there must have been more than a hundred different kinds of food—enormous cans of caviar, more different varieties of smoked fish than I had supposed there were in the world, big steaming chafing dishes filled with hot hors d'œuvres of various kinds, cold and hot meats in such 'profusion that one scarcely knew what to choose. Enough champagne must have been consumed that night to deplete one of the biggest caves in the world. It was excellent French champagne. There was vodka in profusion and Armenian still wines.

I was amazed that the officials would dare serve that sort of dinner in a city where so many people were having difficulty getting food. One of the Russians with whom I talked explained. In the first place, he said, the populace would not know about it; in the second place, if they were told they wouldn't believe it; and in the third place, if they did believe it they would accept the explanation that since the foreigners were all bourgeoisie they must be fed in a bourgeoisie fashion. His explanation sounds fantastic, I admit, but it probably was perfectly correct.

There was nothing light-hearted or gay about the reception—no dancing, of course. Apparently the evening was to be devoted entirely to eating, drinking

and talking. There was plenty of each
of those. But one thing one couldn't fail
to notice was that as the party broke up
around midnight there was not the slightest indication of intoxication on the part
of any of the Russians.

They are a hard drinking people, the
Russians, but they know how to carry
their liquor. Several times during my stay
in Russia I was amazed at the quantity of
vodka the average Russian can consume
without showing it. Vodka, as you probably know, is a drink distilled from potatoes. It has an extremely high alcoholic
content. Your first few drinks taste like
liquid fire; but after a few days one ac-
quires a real liking for it. However, to
the novice, vodka is a dangerous drink.
The reason the Russians can handle it
so well is because the average Russian
never takes a drink without first taking
some food, and each time he takes another drink he takes some more food. The

food acts as a sort of blotter. I sat one night with a Russian friend and between us we consumed almost a quart and a half of vodka and yet neither of us was greatly intoxicated. The answer was in the eating.

Of course, the Russian peasant doesn't follow that plan. He seems to like to drink himself to stupefaction. Walter Duranty told me that during that day he had passed a vodka shop in front of which there were at least a dozen men completely unconscious on the sidewalk or in the gutter. On account of the celebration the government had permitted an extra allowance of vodka. The peasant would go into a shop, buy a quart of vodka, drink it down without leaving the premises. As a matter of fact, after he drank it he couldn't leave the premises, because a quart of that fiery liquid taken without food would almost stupefy a horse.

Russia has no prohibition. You may

buy whatever liquor your ration card permits, but in the shop where you buy it, in the windows of the department stores, on the billboards throughout the streets, there are cartoons and arguments against drinking. There was one especially striking one showing the drunkards being swept out of factories and homes by the intelligent sober workers. The whole plan of the campaign for temperance is to say to the citizen, "You may drink if you want to but you are a fool if you want to."

THE general impression seems to be that churches and religion have been abolished in Russia. That isn't true. They are being abolished; but you still find churches open, there still are priests in them to minister to the spiritual wants of the people. But they are few and far between. In a country where formerly the Church was an integral part of the State, where the Czar was believed to be the direct representative of God, the people are being—and to a great extent, have been—"sold" the belief laid down by Lenin, that "Religion is the opium of the people." The priests have been disfranchised, they have no ration cards; if they subsist it is from the meager offerings which those who still believe can give from their own scant allowances. As a result, only a few are left. Most of the others have been swallowed up in the industrial life of the country. The human will to live is just as strong in their breasts as it is in yours and mine, and when one faces starvation only a few zealots choose to be martyrs.

Anyway, to a great proportion of the Russian populace, there is no God. The younger generation has grown up through a time of war, and after war of Communism. It has seen the destruction of one after another of the beliefs of its forebears. For instance, the Russian of yesterday was told (and in most cases believed) that the bodies of the saints at whose shrines he worshiped never decayed. One of the first steps in the anti-religious movement was to disinter the bones of those saints, and to exhibit them in the anti-religious museums. Little things like that are big factors in propaganda; show that some basic part of any belief is a lie, and you start disintegration in the foundation of that belief. This, is especially true when you deal with mass ignorance on the scale that prevails in Russia.

Now see how that belief can be turned in the opposite direction. In Red Square stands the tomb of Lenin. It was closed for a great part of last year, but fortunately for me it had been opened for the celebration. All day long, from dawn until dusk, long lines of patient people waited from half an hour to an hour to pass through and pay reverence to Lenin.

The day I visited the tomb was cold and raw. Pellets of hard snow stung our faces. If it hadn't been that my companions' press cards entitled us to immediate admittance, I should have given up and returned to the hotel. But there were more than two thousand Russians in the

Square, waiting, shuffling a few feet at a time, waiting again. There was no crowding, no complaining. They must have been terribly uncomfortable, but Russians are so used to discomfort that they didn't seem to mind. They were about evenly divided between men, women and children.

As we went into the tomb, I studied the faces of those about me. Some retained that stolidity so characteristic of the Slav, but most of them seemed alert, eager.

We passed down marble steps, all walking with a funereal slowness, and into a well-lighted chamber. There under a triangular shaped glass case, with vents for air at each end, lay the body of Lenin, probably the most perfect example of the embalmers' craft the world has ever known. He looks for all the world like a middle-aged, rather plump merchant taking an afternoon

[ 65 ]

nap. He is dressed in a khaki-colored uniform. His hands are crossed on his breast. Even the hands seem to retain life, and unless your eyes deceive you, there is a trace of natural color in his cheeks.

The peasants gazed upon him with a reverential awe. We were curious, but they were reverential. As we passed through the exit on the lower floor, I noticed that some of those about us seemed to be murmuring prayers. No need to use much argument to convince those people that there lay the one and only simon-pure saint; the one saint who *didn't* decay. It's a very shrewd job of "selling."

As we returned to the hotel, we could see through the murky light the Cathedral of the Redeemer with its majestic dome made from a ton of pure gold. As I write, that church is being demolished. On its site will be erected a modernistic

Temple of Labor. And there will be no audible protest. For the faith in Communism has become, for most Russians, a fanaticism that exceeds any religious fervor. Instead of a religion based on God, they have a religion based on labor. What boots it then that an edifice known throughout the world shall be torn down, if its place be taken by a monument to the belief of 1931?

## CHAPTER SEVEN

I WAS not molested during my stay in Moscow but I did have considerable difficulty with some of the officials. I wanted to get in contact with the more prominent Russian writers as quickly as possible. I was taken first to the Writers' Union. There I encountered a complicated mass of red tape.

First of all, before anything could be done to get me in touch with the writers, there must be a meeting of the Union at which my object would be explained. I knew this would take more time than I could afford, so I went from there to the offices of the Society for the Promotion of Cultural Relations with Foreign Nations, which long and unhandy name has been contracted into the word Vox.

More red tape. Nothing could be done that day because it was a "rest" day, and the next a holiday. If I would come two days later I might have a talk with some of the officials.

I returned two days later and did have my talk. And then came back another two days later to find out what was to be done.

Vox and the Writers' Union had decided the best method would be to appoint what they called a "collegium" composed of members of the two organizations. This committee would decide what books it would be advisable for me to consider, and when I was ready for publication it would have them translated for me. I was to pay all the expenses of the "collegium."

I hadn't traveled all the way from the United States to have some body of Russians select the material which in their judgment should be fed to the readers in the United States. I tried to make plain that I didn't believe any group of Russians could have a very definite or very intelligent line on the reading taste of the American public; that what I wanted was to find out about the books that had been published recently, meet the writers, make my own arrangements with them and go on my way. I also explained I should want to select my own translator; and, lastly, I had no idea of paying the expenses of a collegium to do my own work.

At this the president of the Vox simply threw up his hands and said my whole project was impossible and indicated that probably the best thing for me to do would be to get out of Russia without further delay.

It happened that I knew what I had set out to do wasn't impossible. I had been very fortunate on the day of my arrival in meeting Charles Malamuth, who had been the instructor in Slavic literature at the University of California. He spoke English and Russian with equal facility. He was ideal for interpreter and translator. We joined forces and began at once on our own to get acquainted with the Russian literature of the day and the Russian writers who seemed to have the greatest possibilities for American publication. We met the writers in their homes, made our deals, and at the end of three weeks I had accomplished all I had come to do.

One of my fears had been that all of the literature which had been produced since the Revolution would be so full of propaganda that it might be unpalatable in the United States. I found that this fear was groundless. While it is true that some of the books are propaganda, many of them are extremely critical of conditions under the present regime. Several books poked fun at the conditions of to-day, and all of those for which I made contracts seemed to me to give the reader not only a good story but an opportunity to understand Russia. Especially, I think the novel, "The Volga Falls to the Caspian Sea," by Boris Pilnyak is a true picture of modern Russia and the Russians of today. Parts of it are almost drastic in their criticism.

There was running at the time a play by Valentine Kataev which, through the medium of farce, brings out the utterly ridiculous situations which sometimes arise from the inadequate housing. It tells the story of two young men living together in a single room. They get married and though this means that four people must occupy that room, cannot get any additional space. Their only way of gaining any privacy is to draw a curtain through the middle of the room and allot one side to each family. One didn't need to understand Russian to appreciate the ludicrous situations which resulted.

It is quite true, however, that most of the plays and motion pictures produced are propaganda. Films from the outside world, with the exception of an occasional Charlie Chaplin or Harold Lloyd of ancient vintage, are not permitted.

The Russian ballet of course is a State institution. I attended a ballet in Moscow and also one in Leningrad. They still have a beauty which surpasses that of any ballet in the world but the costuming is not what it used to be, and it did not seem to me that the members were so well trained as were those whom we have seen in the United States in the past. The Moscow Art Theatre still is in operation and still, I understand, is producing quite extraordinary things, but it was closed at the time I was there.

After having lived in New York and spent some time in several of the European cities, I had a distinct shock at finding myself in a place where there was no night life. Literally there was nothing to do in Moscow after dinner. Once a week there was a wheezy orchestra on the roof garden at the Grand Hotel, but that was attended only by foreigners and there was no place else to go. The restaurants were closed.

In the summer, when the tourists would come under the guidance of Intourist, the bureau which conducts them through the country and lets them see just what it is intended they shall see— and no more—there would be more attempt at gaiety, but while I was there the nights were drab indeed.

Though dull for the visitor, Moscow is a busy place at night. Factories run in three shifts and buildings used for offices in the daytime are turned into schools and colleges at night. There is no time when something in the form of educa-

[ 74 ]

tion is not in progress. Of course, there are workmen's clubs but foreigners are not welcomed at them and even there the only entertainment provided is reading and the eternal talking.

This, despite the fact that theoretically, at least, the Russian with his five-day week has more leisure than any other worker in the world. My impression has been that the five-day week meant that one worked from Monday morning to Friday evening and rested Saturday and Sunday. Not so. The five-day week means that one works at one's job for four days and rests on the fifth. For the visitor the result is confusion. You can't make an engagement for Monday or Tuesday or Wednesday because there is no Monday or Tuesday or Wednesday. You make an engagement for a day of the month.

Everyone has the five-day week, but it doesn't necessarily follow that every

[ 75 ]

member of a family has the same day of rest. The father's day may fall on what to us would be Monday, the mother's on Tuesday and the school children's on Wednesday. Which doesn't increase the congeniality of family life.

One business concern with which you may be dealing may have its day of rest on one day, and another with which you are trying to arrange a part of the same deal may have it on another and a third on still another, so that when you try to get a group of officials together you find that first of all you must determine one day when they all will be at work.

I used the expression that "theo-retically" the Russian worker has more leisure than any other. Actually, at the time I was in Moscow, it was working out something like this. The railroads were terribly congested. Thousands of freight cars with foodstuffs and other necessities were piled up in the yards awaiting unloading. The maid servant of one of the correspondents was notified that on her day of rest she would be expected to volunteer to go to the yards and unload potatoes. A request to volunteer one's services is a command. She went and unloaded potatoes not only that week but for several weeks. And that sort of thing was general throughout the city.

The problem of getting house servants in Moscow presents a lot of difficulties. Each of the correspondents has to have in his home a woman who can act as cook and general housekeeper, and while there is no social distinction against housework there is a distinct prejudice against working for foreigners, and particularly Americans. The fact that in the homes of the correspondents and other Americans there is more food and more comfort than in the Russian homes makes the police feel that the Russian woman working there may get false notions of the things to which she is entitled. Frequently the servant is called up for questioning and while nothing seems to happen as a result of it, it gives her the sort of uncomfortable feeling that very often means that she will prefer some other sort of job.

That espionage also extends to the interpreters. Each of the correspondents, and most of the foreigners, has to have an interpreter constantly. The interpreter, of course, must be a person of some education, must read and write Russian, and be able to understand English. There aren't many persons with those qualifications in Moscow and therefore when a correspondent loses his interpreter he is in quite a fix.

The frequent changing of house servants gets on the nerves of the newcomer. One friend of mine who had been in Moscow only three weeks had changed

that it is a part of the State's duty to give them every possible assistance in birth control. One may go to the State doctors and get instruction and assistance. But at the time the physician not only by speech but with tracts and pamphlets puts up the strongest possible argument against its use. In other words, it's much like their temperance program. They do not say "you may not drink" but they say "you are a fool if you do drink." They do not say "you may not practise birth control" but they try to show you what a great mistake it is. They also make the plea on patriotic grounds, that it is your duty to the State to produce and train children. In dealing with all these questions their plan is to use education rather than prohibition.

I spent one evening in the home of the mother of a friend of mine. This woman had been well off in the old days, but like everyone else had lost what she had during the Revolution and since the Revolution. She and her son and his wife and six children lived in three small rooms. From our standpoint they were far from comfortable rooms. From our standpoint also the food left much to be desired. And yet I knew that they had used up their ration card for several days in order to serve a dinner for me. I have never seen a happier home-life than that in which I found myself that night. Yet, the son and his wife each had been married previously and each of them had three children by the former marriage. The six youngsters played together, and they seemed to me to be more congenial and to have more feeling for each other than most brothers and sisters do.

I talked well into the night with the son about conditions in general and he explained one thing so clearly that I shall pass it on to you. I had asked how it was there was not more discontent when people had to live as he was living.

"Discontent generally comes from jealousy," he said. "With the Russian of today there is little, if any, ground for jealousy. If my neighbor had a bigger place to live in than I have, if he had a radio, a piano, better clothes and better food, I should be jealous of him and I should be discontented. He hasn't any of those things and therefore I am not jealous of him and he is not jealous of me. If the Soviet promise is carried out and eventually I do get more comfort and some luxury, he also will get more at the same time. And since most of the Russians living today have never known anything even slightly approaching luxury, few of them are discontented."

Of course, it would be absurd to say that all Russians have the same income and live in exactly the same manner. That may have been a dream of some of the earlier fanatics, but it just could not work out. Some workers receive as little as thirty rubles a month. Some experts receive as much as 500 a month. Both instances represent exceptions. Members of the Communist party, of whom there are about 2,000,000 including the ruling officials, and of the Communist Youth, about 4,000,000, are limited to a maximum of 300 rubles a month. The average wage throughout the land is in the neighborhood of 100 rubles a month—about $50, in American money. Naturally, the officials, the experts, the heads of industry get a preference in housing, in transportation and such comforts, but the difference is so little that it is of slight moment. The "black worker," that is, the worker with his hands, gets the preference in so many other factors, such as food and clothing and schooling, that he is not inclined to grumble.

Nor is it true that individual effort,

merit and achievement have been stifled.
What you do must be done for the State,
but if you do it well you will be re-
warded. But what you may not do is to
profit by the labor of others. That is why
the class which the correspondents call
"the people who were" are no more.
They were the old ruling and employing
classes. They lived by the toil of others.
Those who are alive and in Russia today
are laboring at whatever jobs the government has allotted to them. But most of
them are not alive. The State took a short
cut to their elimination.

The private farmer is taking the same
route. Lenin encouraged him, but Stalin
has set about deliberately to eliminate
him to make way for collectivized farms
and state farms. If the farmer objects to
the absorption of his farm and his labor,
he finds himself on his way to the Crimea,
to Siberia or to some other far-off place.
He is an outcast. He has no privileges,

[ 85 ]

in many cases not even the privilege of taking his family with him. If he sees the light and works hard to atone for the error of his ways, he may in time be restored to citizenship. If not, well——

The State is All. Its needs are supreme. You get the impression of an enormous machine, relentlessly crushing any individual in its path. Stay out of its path, and it will do much for you. It will provide a doctor to bring your children into the world, it will school them, it will insure them for their old age; it will marry you, divorce you, marry you again. It will promise you more in food and clothing than you may ever have enjoyed before; it will paint you a picture of Utopia just over the hill.

In return you must work at what you are told, where you are told, when you are told. But what is that, from the standpoint of the Russian, who never had his own way anyway, as an exchange for

Hope. What wouldn't a lot of Americans submit to today if they might exchange their unemployment for Hope?

You may have noticed recently that 6,000 skilled American workmen are to leave for Russia between now and early spring. Most of them will take their families with them. The Amtorg, in New York, says that it has applications from close to 100,000 others. There's your answer.

At the conclusion of a talk I made in Detroit after my return, a man in the audience demanded, "Would you like to live there?" No. It's no place for me. They don't need me, don't want me. But if I were an American farmer, growing wheat which I couldn't sell, marketing cattle and hogs for less than it cost me to raise them, I might feel differently. Mightn't you?

ALL through the early part of my life I dreamed of seeing St. Petersburg. To me, it was the most glamorous city in the world. Circumstances made it impossible to realize the dream. But now I was on my way there. At least, I should see what was left of it. And how different what I saw as Leningrad must be from the city that was St. Petersburg, the city Peter the Great built on a marsh and his successors developed into the greatest center of exotic luxury in all the world.

There still is beauty there; but it is the beauty of an old woman. She is wrinkled and defeated, she wears no rouge, her skirts are tattered, her nails

[ 88 ]

unmanicured. You see remnants which show you why she was regarded as a belle in her day, but they're only remnants. She's not the slattern that Moscow is, but she's lost the habit of keeping up appearances.

True, here I found a comfortable suite in the Europsky Hotel; I had fruit and eggs for breakfast and a fair variety from which to choose at other meals; there were carpets on the floors and much more in the way of service than in Moscow, but the city itself tore at my heart.

As I turned for the first time into the Nevsky Prospect, I realized the meaning of the expression "a grandeur that was gone." My companion was an American who had been in Russia off and on for thirty years.

"Just there," he said, "was Cartier's. The shop in Paris was no finer than the one here. Just along there was the Rolls-Royce agency, and right there Mappin

& Webb, with a display of gems such as you wouldn't find anywhere else in the world. All the foremost couturières of Paris had shops. Everywhere along here only the most rare, the most expensive, the most luxurious was on display. Such furs as the world has never known since. Luxury such as probably no other city in the world ever had. There were gorgeous palaces, beautiful theatres, wonderful music. Money was spent on a scale that was staggering. Some of the exclusive restaurants didn't open until midnight, some never closed. The members of the nobility controlled everything; their servants and most of the populace really were serfs. Everything was operated on the theory that the aristocracy could do no wrong. And now look at it."

Yes, look at it. More than half the shops boarded up. The others nothing more than second-hand stores. Some were

called antique shops, but they were second-hand stores just the same. Not a new
article of any sort for sale. Not a new
dress, a new hat, a new pair of shoes.
None of the buildings painted since the
Revolution. Stucco falling from the front
of most of them. Scarcely an automobile
to a city block. Tram cars crowded to the
guards. How I regretted that my visit
had been delayed so many years!

In some of the antique shops you still
find evidences of the old days. In one
dingy salesroom off the Nevsky Prospect, I saw some of the most beautiful
furniture that I ever have beheld—enormous carved chests, beautiful tables and
chairs, armor to make a collector's mouth
water. I could have bought them for a
song and almost did; but just in time I
found how much of a problem it would
be to ship them home. They would be
shipped when there might be a boat on
which all the space was not needed to

send to the rest of the world some of the things which Russia is selling. That might be a month, six months, six years —no one knew. So I had to go away and leave those beautiful things there. Of course, that sort of furniture has no use in Russia any more because no one has sufficient space in which to put it.

I did buy in Moscow a crystal bowl which had belonged to the Czarina, and a tapestry. They were purchased in October and were to be shipped at once. They arrived in New York late in March.

There are many treasures left in Russia. The general impression seems to be that eventually they will come to other countries. Devout Communists say no, that they will be kept for the people; but already there are reports now and then of paintings and sculptures finding their way to Berlin and other markets.

If those in the Hermitage Museum, in Leningrad, ever are put on the market, there will be a feast for collectors. I have been in some of the principal museums of Europe and the United States, but never have I been in one where I saw such a profusion of valuable objects—Rembrandts in number and in beauty greater than in Amsterdam; Van Dyke, all the Dutch masters, and even the English; some of Cellini's work to compare with that in the Metropolitan. And, if the stories one heard are to be believed, hundreds more, taken from the palaces at the time of the Revolution, stored in vaults in the basement.

I spent all of a day in the Hermitage. I could have enjoyed a week there. In fact, I could have enjoyed a month in Leningrad, scraping away the refuse and trying to find that city of my dreams. But it was not to be. My duties called me back to New York. Just at dusk, one evening in November, I took my departure. From the taxi I looked back over the

River Neva, and said to myself, "Well, I'm glad to have seen you even in your decline. I wonder what you'll look like when I come again."

I wonder.

## CHAPTER NINE

THE train reached the border about an hour later. By now it was quite dark. A harsh wind was whistling and snow was crusting the coach windows. It was cold and desolate. There were only four other passengers. None of them spoke English. I had left good friends— friends who spoke Russian, knew the country well, friends who had been my hosts and my guides and my counselors during my stay. I felt lonesome, depressed.

There was nothing to cheer me up at the border. The customs house was a frame building on stilts, about as forbidding a place as you could encounter. On my entrance, soldiers with fixed bayonets ranged on either side of me. I was escorted into a cubby-hole of an office. At a desk sat a uniformed official. He addressed me in Russian. I tried him by answering in English, but he could not understand me any better than I could him. He signaled me to wait. I did, standing against the wall; his was the only chair in the place.

Presently a comparatively young, comparatively blond woman came in. She spoke enough English to make me understand that I was to account for my money. Fortunately, I had all my receipts. They were examined carefully several times, I was told to show the amount of currency I had, and then I was taken to a wicket, where I might change my rubles into Finnish marks. The attendant was figuring the exchange, when I was told to come over for the examination of my luggage. The other passengers had been dismissed and sent to the train. It was quite apparent that I was a special case.

I had taken with me to Russia a number of letters of introduction. One was from Mr. Stimson, our Secretary of State. (Naturally, it was to be used in other countries, not in Russia.) Another was from Senator Borah. (It *was* to be used in Russia, for there he is considered their stanchest American friend.) One was from the officials of the Amtorg, the Russian trading bureau in New York, to their colleagues in Moscow. Others were from American friends to Russian writers. These, with a number of manuscripts by American and English writers, which I had received in Berlin and which I intended to read on my way back to Berlin, I had piled on top the clothing in one of my bags. There were also copies of some contracts I had made with Russian writers.

My first bag was opened. Every article

in it was taken out. Socks were unrolled. Shirts were unfolded. Every pocket was searched. Even the trees were removed from my shoes. And all the disorder was left for me to repair. No one even offered to help me close the bag.

Evidently, they were looking for something, but what? I soon found out.

When the attendant opened the third bag, there was a loud outcry. They had come upon those papers. The comparatively blond interpreter, the inspector, and two or three others grabbed the lot and hurried over to a table where there was a stronger light. The two soldiers stayed with me, one of them still on either side of me. Uncomfortable? Well, rather. I hadn't the slightest idea of what was to come next, but nothing would have surprised me.

The first letter they opened was the one from Secretary Stimson. The interpreter translated it. As she read, I was

the target of some of the blackest scowls
I ever saw, for, as of course you know,
Mr. Stimson is Russia's great bugaboo.

But the next was Senator Borah's letter. That stumped them. Mr. Stimson's
letter might convict me of being a spy,
but Senator Borah's gave me the wings
of an angel. Before going any further
with a puzzle like this, they went into a
sort of huddle.

Meantime, I was wondering how long
that train would wait for me. Every now
and then it would let out a shrill whistle
of impatience. I didn't relish spending
a night in a border jail, or even a border
inn, if there was one. There was one
thing I did know, and that was that it
was no place to start an argument. Not
with my two adhesive-plaster soldiers
still sticking close to me. I decided that
the safest course was to treat the entire
matter, whatever it might be, as a joke.

The interpreter came over to me. In

her faulty English she made clear that it would be necessary for higher officials to read all those papers.

"But I can't wait all that time," I protested; "I have a lot of important engagements in Stockholm and Copenhagen and Berlin. You surely don't want to keep a busy man around here, looking at what you call scenery while you do all that reading. Anyway, they are only manuscripts of short stories and novels, and I don't think you'd enjoy them."

"That's what you say," she answered, and went back to the inspector. They held another consultation. They looked me over. They examined my other bag, and found nothing incriminating. I had some things I was bringing from Russia, but I had the export licenses for all of them. This seemed to impress them a bit.

Remembering the injunction in the advertisements, I had lighted a cigarette and was looking as nonchalant as I could

[100]

under the circumstances. Also meantime, the engineer of the train was showing what he thought of the delay by blasting the night air with toots from the whistle.

Another consultation. Then the interpreter explained that they had decided to let me proceed, but that I must leave my papers with them. I did not mind about the manuscripts or the letters, but I did hate to leave those contracts. I was afraid for the authors who had made them without consulting Vox or the Union. However, there was nothing else to do. So I took a chance on another joke.

"There's just one thing I ask," I said to the interpreter. "Ask each person who reads them to pencil on the margin whether he thinks the story is any good. That may save my reading them."

That one penetrated. She laughed. She translated it to the inspector. He laughed. So did the soldiers. I felt much better, as I gave them the address to which to send the papers when they were through with them. I repacked my bags, and carried them one by one down the steps leading to the train platform— about ten steps. Just as I reached the bottom of the steps with the last one, a terrific hullabaloo broke out behind me. The door burst open, and my two soldiers came at me pell mell.

"Well," I said to myself, "I guess this is where I get it after all. My humor wasn't as good as I thought it was."

But when they reached me, it developed that what was amiss was that in the discussion and confusion over the luggage, I had left my Finnish marks at the change wicket, and they had just discovered it. I tried to tip them for their trouble, but they refused, and as I staggered onto the train, the interpreter, the inspector and my two soldiers waved me a farewell. (In parenthesis, let me state that ten days later, in Berlin, all my papers came back to me. But they didn't put the penciled notations on the manuscripts, as I had requested.)

The impatient engineer hardly waited for me to settle in my seat before we were under way. Twenty minutes later, we were in Finland. I went into a brightly-lighted, clean station, and into a dining-room where pleasant-faced waitresses served me delicious roast beef, crisp, clean salad, excellent beer, and a piece of pastry such as legend says mother used to make. And coffee, real coffee. Junius Wood had done well with the coffee he so kindly gave me, but this was *real* coffee. And if you love coffee as I do, and have been without the real article as long as I had, you'll know just what that meant to me. I don't think I ever ate as much at one sitting, and I know I never enjoyed a meal more.

As I went out to board the train, I looked back toward Russia. I visualized

again that relentless machine. I hadn't
got in its path, but I had felt a draft as it
whizzed by me.

"A wonderful experience," I said to
myself, "but——"

TWENTY-FOUR hours later, sitting before a window in the Grand Hotel, in Stockholm, looking out over that beautiful harbor toward the palace across the way, I wrote to myself:

"From what I have seen of Russia, I am convinced that what happens there in the next twenty years will have more effect on the future of my seven-year-old son than anything I can do for him or with him.

"That what happens there will more seriously affect the future of my country than any other factor.

"That what happens there will more nearly shape the history of the world than any other factor.

[105]

"That Russia today—and certainly to-morrow—presents the greatest economic menace to the United States, to England, to Canada, to the Argentine, perhaps to Germany and France, that any of those countries ever has faced.

"And that the future of the world depends on the intelligence with which the various countries meet it.

"And that as soon as I can I want to go back and see what's happening. I don't want to live there. God forbid. But I have seen part of the most extraordinary movement that it has so far been permitted man to see, and I want to watch its progress at frequent intervals through whatever years it may be allotted me to live."

That is just what I feel today.

The rest of the world, and particularly the United States, must quit kidding itself. It must quit thinking of Communists as long-haired, crackbrained, dirty-finger-nailed agitators who sometimes make fiery speeches in public places in our cities so that unintelligent policemen may make martyrs of them by hitting them over their heads with clubs. That isn't Russia. Stalin and his Georgians, stalwart, husky, intelligent, shrewd economists and shrewd politicians—they are the Russia we've got to consider.

On the State farms and on the collective farms they grow a bushel of wheat and load it on a vessel headed for its destination at a total cost of less than 15 cents. We have heard a lot about wheat dumping in the last year or so, but the wheat that Russia has exported so far is not equal to what she exported before the War, when she was the greatest wheat-growing nation in the world, and it is nothing to what she is planning to export. So far as I can see, we can't stop her.

In the old days the Russian peasant

farmer tilled his soil with a forked stick with a piece of steel welded on the point. Today his farm may be part of a State farm or a collective farm where a fleet of a hundred tractors, with rotary plows attached to them, dig a furrow twenty miles in one direction, twenty miles in another direction, twenty miles back, and in almost no time have under modern cultivation a wheat field of 400 square miles.

We in the United States may rail at this all we want, but if we content ourselves with railing we shall be in exactly the same position as the ostrich is when he sticks his head in the sand and thinks that he is hidden. Russia can grow wheat cheaper than we possibly can. Russia is going to grow that wheat. She is going to sell it to the outside world. Since we can't compete with Russia, it seems to me only logical that we should teach our farmers to grow something other than wheat. If we grow wheat only for our own consumption and devote the rest of our energies to growing other things we can compete with them. If we don't, we can't.

Russia has vast stores of ore. She will be one of the big producers of steel. She has unlimited water-power. She will be a vast manufacturer. She can grow cotton, flax; she can raise wool. Russia probably is the greatest *potential* producer in the world. She won't achieve her potentialities over night. It will require years to teach untrained, clumsy hands to utilize instead of ruining machinery, to overcome ignorance and transmute it into skill. But each day that Sovietism endures is a step toward those goals.

The point we seem to overlook is that Russia not only is going to be one of the big *selling* nations of the world, but as it sells and receives money for its products, it must be one of the big *pur-*

*chasing* nations. Our plan seems to be to ignore Russia, to shut our eyes, to say we won't sell Russia anything because its money must be tainted. Other countries are not taking that attitude. Therefore, it seems to me logical that our attitude, instead of being what it is should be that if Russia can sell wheat cheaper than we can, let her sell wheat and that for the money she receives from wheat, we will sell her some of the things we produce and she needs. Remember that *if* Stalin's plans succeed, Russia may be one of the big purchasers of luxuries before long.

How anyone can justify a recent incident is beyond me. The Amtorg, which is the Russian purchasing agency in the United States, wanted to buy 200,000 bales of cotton. Our cotton planters in the South are in the midst of depression even greater than that in other parts of the country, but our government said, "No, we won't sell that cotton to them. Their credit isn't any good, and anyway, they are a bad lot. We don't want their money."

If we simply maintain that attitude long enough we shall awaken one day and find that the Russians have taken a lot of our export trade and that we have nothing in return. In fact, they are taking that trade steadily day by day now and we are getting nothing in return. We are sending them experts to guide them in the paths that will lead them to stronger competition with us. We are sending them railroad men, engineers, electrical experts, all sorts of expert instruction, but still we do not seem to be able to realize that those factors are going to mean anything to the citizens of the United States.

I think the chief trouble is that the average American citizen, and especially the average American business man, thinks that if we trade with Russia we are encouraging bolshevism and, of course, the word bolshevik is a bugaboo which will frighten any American business man.

There wasn't much question that Lenin and his immediate followers did have the desire and the intention to try to convert the rest of the world to Communism. Frankly, I don't think the present regime cares a continental what happens in the rest of the world. I think that they and their followers have had time now to realize that while the Soviet system of government may be an excellent thing for Russia, it probably would not apply to any other country, except possibly China or India. They certainly must know that they have slight chance of ever making any noticeable progress in the United States. Anyway, the Soviet government has its hands too full trying to carry out its five-year plan

and its plans for the much more remote
future to worry about trying to convert
the rest of us.

Russia works while we sleep. She has
no unemployment; she has a labor shortage. She has not much money and her
credit isn't good, but she is getting more
money and getting more credit all the
time. We may consider that money
tainted because we say it was produced
by a form of convict labor, and we may
not want to extend credit to her because
she has repudiated her debts, but when
I think of the number of unemployed in
my own country who might be at work
...d who might therefore be prospective
customers for your wares and mine, it
makes me wonder.

I came away from Russia feeling dis-
couraged about the world in general. I
had gone in through Germany and had
seen the fix the Germans were in, and I
came out through Finland and Sweden

and Denmark and saw a contrast. Those Scandinavian countries are trading with Russia. They are selling them everything they can and in Scandinavia you see real prosperity. The Russian money may be tainted, but the Scandinavians see in it as much buying power as there is in any other money.

I reached New York just before Christmas. A pretty gloomy Christmas, that of 1930. One night between Christmas and New Year's I was making my way around Columbus Circle. There was a bread line, one of many in New York. It was as long as some of the waiting lines I had seen in Russia.

There was one difference. Those in the line in New York were waiting for charity. Those in line in Russia were waiting to *buy*.

That's a big difference. A difference which may warrant your serious consideration.

[114]